5/20

About Seabirds

A Guide for Children

Cathryn Sill

Illustrated by John Sill

PEACHTREE

ATLANTA

For the One who created seabirds.

—*Genesis* 1:20

Published by
PEACHTREE PUBLISHING COMPANY INC.
1700 Chattahoochee Avenue
Atlanta, Georgia 30318-2112
www.peachtree-online.com

Text © 2020 by Cathryn P. Sill
Illustrations © 2020 by John C. Sill

Edited by Vicky Holifield

Illustrations created in watercolor on archival quality 100% rag watercolor paper
Text and titles typeset in Novarese from Adobe Systems

Printed in February 2020 by Toppan Leefung in China
10 9 8 7 6 5 4 3 2 1
First Edition

ISBN 978-1-68263-092-1

Library of Congress Cataloging-in-Publication Data

Names: Sill, Cathryn P., 1953– author. | Sill, John, illustrator.
Title: About seabirds : a guide for children / written by Cathryn Sill ; illustrated by John Sill.
Description: First edition. | Atlanta : Peachtree Publishers, [2020] | Audience: Ages 3–7. | Audience: Grade K to 3.
Identifiers: LCCN 2019019069 | ISBN 9781682630921
Subjects: LCSH: Seabirds—Juvenile literature.
Classification: LCC QL678.52 .S55 2020 | DDC 598.177—dc23 LC record available at
https://lccn.loc.gov/2019019069

About Seabirds

Seabirds are birds that live on or near the ocean.

A few live on lakes.

Some seabirds live along the shore and never get far from land.

PLATE 3
Brown Pelican

Others spend very long periods of time without coming to land.

Most seabirds have waterproof feathers that keep them warm and dry.

Some need to dry their feathers when they get wet.

Seabirds eat mostly fish or other animals such as krill, squid, or crustaceans.

Some hunt for food by plunging into the water from high in the air.

Others dive and chase their
prey underwater.

Some grab food from the surface of the water.

A few get food by stealing from
other seabirds.

Many seabirds migrate long distances to find food and raise their young.

PLATE 12
Arctic Tern

Most seabirds nest in large groups called "colonies."

Some seabirds build nests from materials
such as mud and grass, sticks, rocks,
or seaweed.

PLATE 14
a. Grey-headed Albatross
b. Red-footed Booby
c. Adélie Penguin
d. Flightless Cormorant

Others nest in burrows.

PLATE 15
Grey Petrel

Some do not build a nest at all.

Seabirds need clean, healthy oceans.

PLATE 17
Laysan Albatross

It is important to protect seabirds and the places where they live.

PLATE 18
Razorbill

Afterword

PLATE 1

There are more than 325 species of seabirds in oceans all over the world. They live in different environments from cold polar oceans to warm tropical waters. Seabirds are so adapted to life at sea that many of them cannot walk well on land. Shearwaters spend most of the time on the open ocean. They get their name by flying so close to the water that their wingtips sometimes "cut" or "shear" the surface. Great Shearwaters live over cold water in the Atlantic and southwestern Indian Oceans.

PLATE 2

Some seabirds nest on lakes and other bodies of fresh water. After their young are raised they may move to the coasts to spend the winter. Some Ring-billed Gulls never visit the sea. Ring-billed Gulls will eat almost anything. They often live near people and search for food in garbage dumps, fast-food parking lots, and freshly plowed fields where they look for worms or other small animals. Ring-billed Gulls are common in North America, both inland and on beaches.

PLATE 3

Seabirds that live close to land usually hunt for fish by flying or swimming just offshore. They sometimes gather in large groups on the beach or on piers and docks. Some coastal seabirds, including Brown Pelicans, sleep on land. Brown Pelicans dive headfirst from the air into the water to catch fish. They live along the Atlantic and Pacific coasts of North and South America.

PLATE 4

Seabirds that spend most of their time away from land are called "pelagic birds." Some of them soar for days at a time. Pelagic birds have a special way to lock their wings open to keep from getting tired. These birds can sleep for short periods of time while flying and sometimes rest by floating on the water. Albatrosses can fly for thousands of miles (kilometers) without stopping. Wandering Albatrosses live in the Southern Ocean. They have the longest wingspan (11.5 feet or 3.5 meters) of any bird.

PLATE 5

Seabirds have more feathers than land birds. A thick coat of soft downy feathers underneath the outer feathers protects seabirds from their cold wet environment. Most seabirds make their feathers waterproof with oil from a gland near the base of their tail. They spread the oil by preening their feathers and rubbing the oil over them. Penguins can preen in the water and on land. King Penguins live in the subantarctic region.

PLATE 6

A few seabirds have feathers that soak up water. The feathers are heavier when wet and help birds such as cormorants and shags dive deeper as they hunt for fish. After eating, they come to land and spread their wings to let the waterlogged feathers dry. Pied Cormorants live in Australia and New Zealand. They live along the coast and on larger inland waters.

PLATE 7

Seabirds eat and drink a lot of salt as they hunt in the ocean. Salt glands near their eyes help them get rid of the extra salt, which then drains through nostrils on their bills. Seabirds have different shaped bills to help them catch the kind of food they need. Puffins have special ridges in their mouth that allow them to hold several fish in place while they catch more. Atlantic Puffins live on the Atlantic Ocean from North America to Europe.

PLATE 8

Birds that plunge-dive for their food drop headfirst into the water from high in the air. Some seabirds such as gannets have special nostrils inside their bill to keep water out when they dive. They also have inner eyelids called "nictitating membranes" that protect their eyes as they hit the water. Northern Gannets usually dive from heights of 16 to 130 feet (5 to 40 meters). They live in the Atlantic Ocean north of the equator.

PLATE 9

Birds that chase their prey underwater (pursuit diving birds) use their wings and feet to swim. Some use their wings as paddles and their feet to steer. Others push through the water using mainly their feet. Pigeon Guillemots use their feet and short sturdy wings as they chase small fish. Pigeon Guillemots live in the northern Pacific Ocean.

PLATE 10

Some surface feeders hunt by sitting on the water and picking up small fish, shrimp, or plankton (tiny floating animals and plants) that are swimming near the top. Others fly or hover over the ocean so they can snatch food at the surface of the water. Wilson's Storm Petrels often patter their feet on the surface of the water to stir up plankton. They are common in oceans all around the world.

PLATE 11

Animals that steal food from other animals are called "kleptoparasites." These seabirds chase and harass other birds until they throw up or drop their recent catch. The thief swoops down and grabs a meal. Magnificent Frigatebirds get some food by stealing. They also catch flying fish or pick up fish at the surface of the ocean. Their feathers are not waterproof, so they must be careful to stay dry. Magnificent Frigatebirds live on both coasts of North and South America and in the Caribbean Sea.

PLATE 12

Most seabirds wander over hundreds of miles (kilometers) searching for food. Some fly long distances to their nesting grounds when it is time to raise babies. They search for food that is closer to their nests when they are feeding young. After their chicks are grown, many seabirds migrate thousands of miles (kilometers). Arctic Terns migrate farther than any other animal. They fly from their breeding grounds in the Arctic to Antarctica and back again each year.

PLATE 13

Seabird colonies are usually located on remote places such as islands or cliffs. This helps protect their chicks from predators. When birds nest close together in large groups, it is easier for them to spot danger. Blue-footed Boobies lay eggs in a scraped-out place on the ground. Boobies and many other seabirds perform an elaborate dance called a "courtship display" during the breeding season. Blue-footed Boobies live in tropical areas of the eastern Pacific Ocean.

PLATE 14

Most seabirds return to the same nest site year after year. Grey-headed Albatrosses build mud nests lined with grass on subantarctic islands in the Southern Ocean. Red-footed Boobies build stick nests in low bushes or shrubs on islands in tropical oceans around the world. Adélie Penguins build nests from pebbles on the Antarctic coast and on nearby islands. Flightless Cormorants use seaweed to build nests on the Galapagos Islands, Ecuador.

PLATE 15

Seabirds that nest underground make or find burrows in the soil or build nests in small caves in rocky places. Grey Petrels dig into steep slopes covered with bunches of grass and other plants. They feed their chicks by regurgitating (bringing up swallowed food) fish and squid. Grey Petrels live in southern oceans around the world.

PLATE 16

Some seabirds lay eggs right on rocky ledges or on the ground. White Terns lay their eggs on bare branches, usually near a fork or in a dent in the tree trunk. The chicks have strong feet to help them hang on to the branch. White Terns nest on islands in tropical and subtropical oceans around the world.

PLATE 17

Pollution caused by oil spills, chemicals, and plastic garbage threatens the lives of many seabirds. Oil destroys the waterproofing on seabirds' feathers. This causes them to get wet and cold. Swallowing oil and chemicals as they clean their feathers can poison them. Many seabirds mistake floating plastic for food. Eating it or feeding it to their young is dangerous. Many chicks die each year because of the plastic in their stomachs. Laysan Albatrosses live in the northern Pacific Ocean.

PLATE 18

Pollution is not the only threat to seabirds. People have introduced animals such as cats and rats to islands with seabird colonies. These alien species raid the nests and eat the eggs or chicks. Many seabirds are caught and killed by fishing gear. Overfishing leaves fewer fish for seabirds. Climate change is causing conditions in the ocean that may make it hard for seabirds to find their usual food. People have used seabirds such as Razorbills for meat, eggs, and feathers. Razorbills live across the North Atlantic Ocean.

GLOSSARY

alien species—animals or plants that are not native
breeding season—the time when animals mate and raise young
equator—an imaginary line around the middle of the earth halfway between the North and South Poles
hover—staying in one place in the air
patter—repeated light tapping
pollution—anything that makes water, air, or land unclean or impure
predator—an animal that lives by hunting and eating other animals
prey—an animal that is hunted and eaten by a predator
species—a group of animals or plants that are alike in many ways

SUGGESTIONS FOR FURTHER READING

BOOKS

ZOOBOOKS SEABIRDS by Beth Wagner Brust and Marjorie Betts Shaw (Wildlife Education Ltd).

WEBSITES

"Birdlife International," *www.birdlife.org/europe-and-central-asia/programmes/seabirds-and-marine*
"Classic Collection of North American Birds," *www.birds-of-north-america.net/seabirds.html*
"The Cornell Lab," *www.allaboutbirds.org/guide/browse/shape/Seabirds*

RESOURCES ESPECIALLY HELPFUL IN DEVELOPING THIS BOOK

FAR FROM LAND: THE MYSTERIOUS LIVES OF SEABIRDS by Michael Brooke (Princeton University Press)
HANDBOOK OF THE BIRDS OF THE WORLD: Vols. 1 and 3 Edited by Josep del Hoyo, Andrew Elliott, Jordi Sargatal
    (Lynx Edicions, Barcelona)
SEABIRDS OF THE WORLD: THE COMPLETE REFERENCE by Jim Enticott and David Tipling (Stackpole Books)

ABOUT... SERIES

About Amphibians
HC: 978-1-68263-031-0
PB: 978-1-68263-032-7

About Arachnids
HC: 978-1-56145-038-1
PB: 978-1-56145-364-1

About Birds
HC: 978-1-56145-688-8
PB: 978-1-56145-699-4

About Crustaceans
HC: 978-1-56145-301-6
PB: 978-1-56145-405-1

About Fish
HC: 978-1-56145-987-2
PB: 978-1-56145-988-9

About Hummingbirds
HC: 978-1-56145-588-1
PB: 978-1-56145-837-0

About Insects
HC: 978-1-56145-881-3
PB: 978-1-56145-882-0

About Mammals
HC: 978-1-56145-757-1
PB: 978-1-56145-758-8

About Marine Mammals
HC: 978-1-56145-906-3

About Marsupials
HC: 978-1-56145-358-0
PB: 978-1-56145-407-5

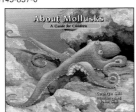

About Mollusks
PB: 978-1-56145-406-8

About Parrots
HC: 978-1-56145-795-3
PB: 978-1-68263-158-4

About Penguins
HC: 978-1-56145-743-4
PB: 978-1-56145-741-0

About Raptors
HC: 978-1-56145-536-2
PB: 978-1-56145-811-0

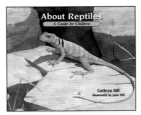

About Reptiles
HC: 978-1-56145-907-0
PB: 978-1-56145-908-7

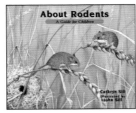

About Rodents
HC: 978-1-56145-454-9
PB: 978-1-56145-914-8

About Woodpeckers
HC: 978-1-68263-004-4

ALSO AVAILABLE IN BILINGUAL
AND SPANISH EDITIONS

- About Amphibians / Sobre los anfibios / 978-1-68263-033-4 PB ● About Birds / Sobre los pájaros / 978-1-56145-783-0 PB
- About Fish / Sobre los peces / 978-1-56145-989-6 PB ● About Insects / Sobre los insectos / 978-1-56145-883-7 PB
- About Mammals / Sobre los mamíferos / 978-1-56145-800-4 PB ● About Reptiles / Sobre los reptiles / 978-1-56145-909-4 PB

- Sobre los insectos / 978-1-68263-155-3 PB ● Sobre los mamíferos / 978-1-68263-072-3 PB
- Sobre los pájaros / 978-1-68263-071-6 PB ● Sobre los peces / 978-1-68263-154-6 PB

HC: 978-1-56145-641-3
PB: 978-1-56145-636-9

HC: 978-1-56145-734-2
PB: 978-1-68263-126-3

HC: 978-1-56145-559-1
PB: 978-1-68263-034-1

HC: 978-1-56145-469-3
PB: 978-1-56145-731-1

HC: 978-1-56145-618-5
PB: 978-1-56145-960-5

HC: 978-1-56145-832-5

HC: 978-1-68263-091-4

HC: 978-1-56145-968-1

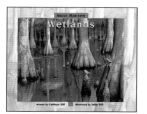

HC: 978-1-56145-432-7
PB: 978-1-56145-689-5

THE SILLS

CATHRYN AND JOHN SILL are the dynamic team who created the *About…* series as well as the *About Habitats* series. Their books have garnered praise from educators and have won a variety of awards, including Bank Street Best Books, CCBC Choices, NSTA/CBC Outstanding Science Trade Books for Students K–12, Orbis Pictus Recommended, and *Science Books and Films* Best Books of the Year. Cathryn, a graduate of Western Carolina State University, taught early elementary school classes for thirty years. John holds a BS in wildlife biology from North Carolina State University. Combining his artistic skill and knowledge of wildlife, he has achieved an impressive reputation as a wildlife artist. The Sills live in Franklin, North Carolina.

Fred Eldredge, Creative Image Photography